I Know Someone with
Diabetes

Vic Parker

Heinemann Library
Chicago, Illinois

www.heinemannraintree.com
Visit our website to find out more information about Heinemann-Raintree books.

To order:
☎ Phone 888-454-2279
🖳 Visit www.heinemannraintree.com
to browse our catalog and order online.

Edited by Rebecca Rissman, Daniel Nunn, and Siân Smith
Designed by Joanna Hinton Malivoire
Picture research by Mica Brancic
Originated by Capstone Global Library
Printed in the United States of America by Worzalla Publishing

14 13 12 11 10
10 9 8 7 6 5 4 3 2 1

Library of Congress Cataloging-in-Publication Data
Parker, Victoria.
  I know someone with diabetes / Vic Parker.
    p. cm. — (Understanding health issues)
  Includes bibliographical references and index.
  ISBN 978-1-4329-4557-2 (hc)
  ISBN 978-1-4329-4573-2 (pb)
  1. Diabetes—Juvenile literature. I. Title.
  RC660.5.P39 2011
  616.4'62—dc22   2010026418

Acknowledgments
We would like to thank the following for permission to reproduce photographs: Alamy pp. 15 (© ACE Stock Limited), 16 (© Anne-Marie Palmer), 17 (© Martin Shields); Getty Images pp. 18 (PhotoAlto Agency RF Collections/Odilon Dimier), 27 (AFP Photo/Thomas Coex); Getty Images Entertainment p. 26 (Jemal Countess); iStockphoto pp. 6 (© Steve Debenport), 13 (© Aldo Murillo), 20 (© Cristian Lazzari), 21 (© Christopher Futcher), 23 (© Radu Razvan); Photolibrary pp. 4 (Radius Images), 5 (Uppercut Images RF/ Jay Reilly), 7 (Photoalto/Laurence Mouton), 8 (age fotostock/Javier Larrea), 9 (imagebroker.net/Martin Moxter), 10 (OJO Images/Sam Edwards), 11 (Banana Stock), 14 (BSIP Medical/May May), 19 (Index Stock Imagery/Robert Ginn), 22 (BSIP Medical/Jose Oto), 25 (Image Source); Shutterstock p. 12 (© Maga).

Cover photograph of a couple and their daughter cooking reproduced with permission of Getty Images (Photodisc/Jack Hollingsworth).

We would like to thank Matthew Siegel and Ashley Wolinski for their invaluable help in the preparation of this book.

Every effort has been made to contact copyright holders of any material reproduced in this book. Any omissions will be rectified in subsequent printings if notice is given to the publisher.

All the Internet addresses (URLs) given in this book were valid at the time of going to press. However, due to the dynamic nature of the Internet, some addresses may have changed, or sites may have changed or ceased to exist since publication. While the author and publisher regret any inconvenience this may cause readers, no responsibility for any such changes can be accepted by either the author or the publisher.

Contents

Do You Know Someone with Diabetes? 4

What Is Type 1 Diabetes? 6

How Do You Get Type 1 Diabetes? 8

A Different Type of Diabetes 10

The Causes of Type 2 Diabetes 12

Living with Type 1 Diabetes 14

Living with Type 2 Diabetes 16

What Is "Going Low"? 18

Food Choices 20

About Blood Testing 22

Being a Good Friend 24

Famous People with Diabetes 26

Diabetes: Facts and Fiction 28

Glossary *30*

Find Out More *31*

Index *32*

Some words are printed in bold, **like this**. You can find out what they mean in the glossary.

Do You Know Someone with Diabetes?

You might have a friend with diabetes mellitus, often just called "diabetes." Diabetes is a **medical condition**. This means that a doctor must tell your friend things to do to stay healthy.

You cannot catch diabetes.

Someone with diabetes can wear a bracelet or necklace to let others know.

You cannot tell that people have diabetes just by looking at them. There is nothing to see. This is because diabetes happens on the inside of someone's body, not the outside.

What Is Type 1 Diabetes?

When we eat, our bodies make something inside us called **insulin**. Insulin helps turn the sugar we get from certain foods into **energy**, so that we can run and jump and play.

Sugar comes from foods such as bread, bananas, sweets, and pasta.

Too much sugar in your blood can make you feel very tired, thirsty, and unwell.

When young people get Type 1 diabetes, their bodies stop making insulin. This means their bodies cannot turn sugar from food into energy. Instead, the sugar builds up in their blood and makes them unwell.

How Do You Get Type 1 Diabetes?

No one is sure why young people get Type 1 diabetes. Some children who develop it have an older relative with Type 1 diabetes, too. Others suddenly get it after a bad illness.

Many scientists are working to discover what causes Type 1 diabetes.

Young people with diabetes can join groups or go on outings where they can have fun and meet other people with diabetes.

Most young people who get Type 1 diabetes are between the ages of 10 and 14. However, some are even younger. Once you get Type 1 diabetes, you have it for the rest of your life.

A Different Type of Diabetes

Many more adults than young people get diabetes. Adults usually develop a different version of the **medical condition**. This is called Type 2 diabetes.

Many people have grandparents with Type 2 diabetes.

People with Type 2 diabetes still make **insulin** in their bodies. However, this insulin either does not work as well as it should, or there is not enough of it.

Sugar can build up in the blood of someone with Type 2 diabetes, just as it can for someone with Type 1 diabetes.

The Causes of Type 2 Diabetes

Exercising and eating healthily can help everyone to stay well.

Adults can get Type 2 diabetes if they are overweight. This is often because they have made unhealthy food choices and have not exercised regularly.

Adults are more likely to get Type 2 diabetes if relatives have it, too. People from certain **ethnic** backgrounds, such as African Americans, South Asians, or Hispanics, are also more likely to develop Type 2 diabetes.

You might be surprised by how many adults you know who have Type 2 diabetes.

Living with Type 1 Diabetes

People with Type 1 diabetes need to take **insulin** as medicine. Then their bodies can turn the sugar from food into **energy**, and they feel well. They have up to five **injections** of insulin every day.

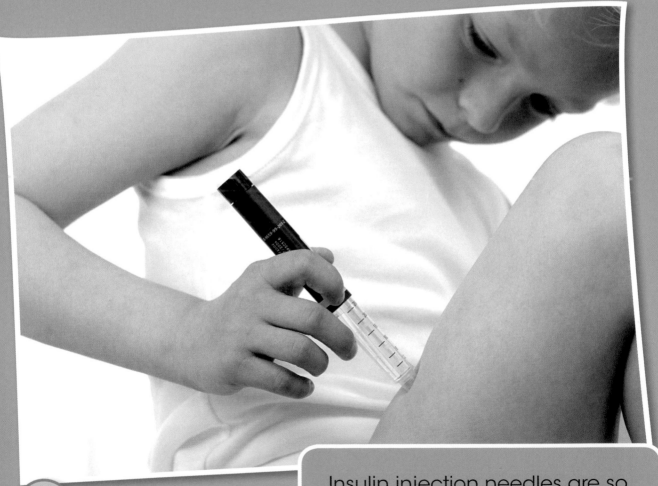

Insulin injection needles are so small you can hardly feel them.

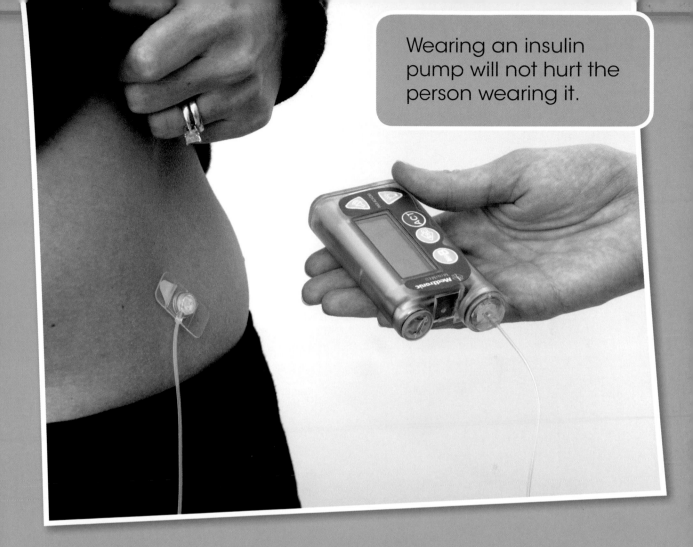

Wearing an insulin pump will not hurt the person wearing it.

Other people with Type 1 diabetes use an insulin pump. This clips onto their clothes while a tiny needle stays in their skin. People can sleep, shower, and even swim wearing an insulin pump.

Living with Type 2 Diabetes

Many people with Type 2 diabetes can take tablets as treatment. These tablets either get the body to make enough **insulin**, or they help the body's insulin to work better.

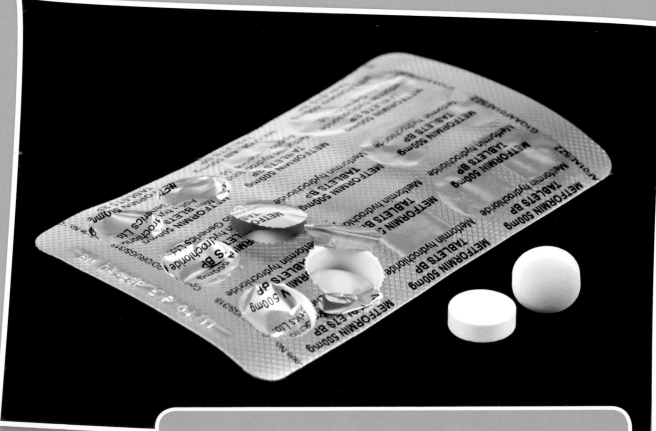

You can help friends with Type 2 diabetes by reminding them to take their medicine.

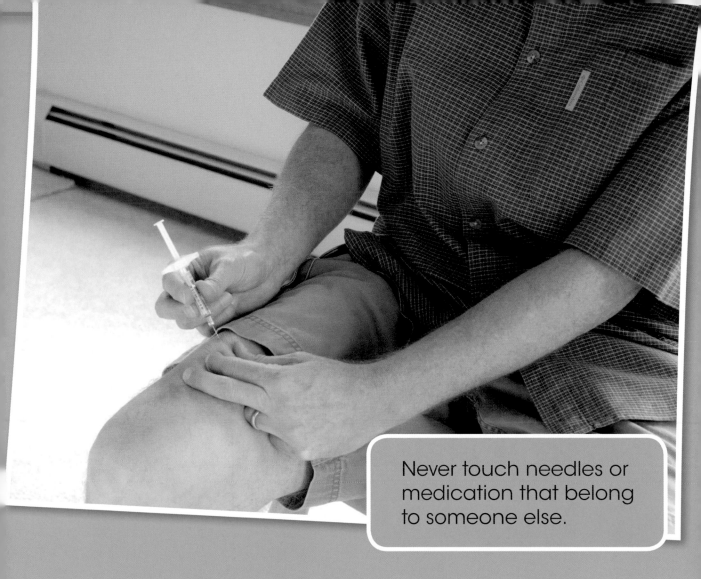

Never touch needles or medication that belong to someone else.

Some people with Type 2 diabetes have **injections**. These may contain a medicine that works the same way that tablets do. Or they may use injections of insulin.

What Is "Going Low"?

Sometimes, people with diabetes may turn pale and become shaky, confused, or grumpy. This means all the sugar from their food has been turned into **energy** and used up. It is called "**going low**."

You may realize that friends with diabetes are "going low" before they realize it themselves.

People with low blood sugar need a sugary drink or some sugary sweets right away. They should soon feel better. If they do not, you can help by calling an ambulance urgently.

If people with low blood sugar do not have sugar quickly enough, they may pass out and have a **seizure**.

Food Choices

To stay well, people with diabetes should eat regular, small amounts of starchy foods at meal and snack times. Starchy foods include potatoes, rice, pasta, and bread.

Bananas are a tasty starchy food.

We should all make healthy food choices to stay well.

People with diabetes should usually avoid sugary foods, but eat lots of vegetables and **whole foods**. They should not skip meals or healthy snacks. People without diabetes should also do these things to eat healthily.

About Blood Testing

If people with diabetes do not follow their doctors' instructions, the amount of sugar in their blood may rise too high. This can harm different body parts, such as the eyes and **nerves**.

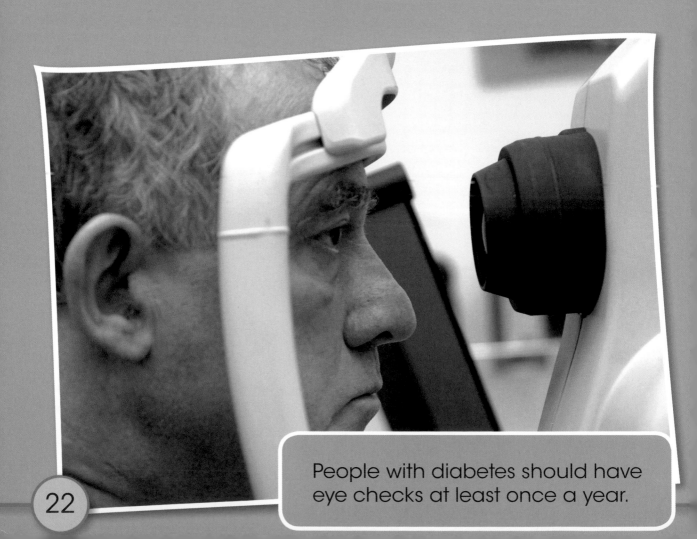

People with diabetes should have eye checks at least once a year.

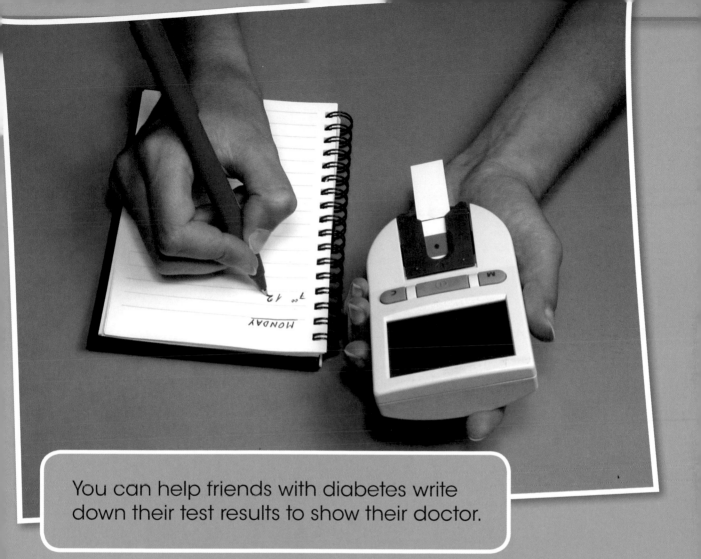

You can help friends with diabetes write down their test results to show their doctor.

People with diabetes can check how much sugar is in their blood by using a special machine. This can help them to keep their blood sugar level just right, so that they stay healthy.

Being a Good Friend

There are many ways you can be a good friend to people with diabetes. You can:

- try not to think of your friend as "sick"
- help each other to exercise
- carry a sugary drink in case your friend **"goes low"**
- make healthy food choices with your friend.

We all have different bodies and different personalities.

Living with diabetes can be difficult at times. We are all different in many ways. A good friend likes us and values us for who we are.

Famous People with Diabetes

Nick Jonas wears an **insulin** pump to manage his diabetes.

Nick Jonas got Type 1 diabetes at the age of 13. It has not stopped him from becoming a popular singer and actor with his own television show.

Steve Redgrave is one of the greatest Olympic athletes of all time.

Steve Redgrave was already a champion rower when he developed Type 1 diabetes. He worked hard to manage the **medical condition** and won gold medals at five Olympic Games!

Diabetes: Facts and Fiction

Facts

- Experts guess about 5 million Americans have Type 2 diabetes without knowing it yet.

- At least 171 million people in the world have diabetes.

Fiction

(?) Eating lots of sugar-free sweets and chocolate is a good idea.

WRONG! These foods can still raise blood sugar and can give you a stomachache and diarrhea.

(?) People with diabetes should never eat sugary foods and drinks.

WRONG! People with diabetes may need to eat some sugary stuff at certain times, such as if they exercise, or if they are "**going low**."

Glossary

energy power to do something. We use energy when we run, jump, and play.

ethnic belonging to a certain race of people

going low when someone suddenly has low blood sugar (not enough sugar in the blood)

injection needle that puts medicine into a person's body

insulin liquid made in our bodies that controls the amount of sugar in our blood

medical condition health problem that a person has for a long time or for life

nerves long, fine threads that carry information between body parts and the brain

seizure disturbance in someone's brain, which can affect the person's senses, behavior, feelings, or thoughts for a while

whole food food that is kept as natural as possible, without having things added or taken away from it

Find Out More

Books to read

Bryan, Jenny. *I Have Diabetes* (*Taking Care of Myself*). New York: Gareth Stevens, 2011.

Glaser, Jason. *Juvenile Diabetes* (*First Facts*). Mankato, Minn.: Capstone, 2007.

Powell, Jillian. *Becky Has Diabetes* (*Like Me, Like You*). Langhorne, Pa.: Chelsea Clubhouse, 2005.

Websites

http://kidshealth.org/kid/centers/diabetes_center.html
Visit Kids' Health to watch an animation that helps you learn about Type 1 and Type 2 diabetes.

www.diabetes.org
The American Diabetes Association website has information, recipes, and more for people who have diabetes.

Index

adults with diabetes 8, 10, 12–13

blood testing 22–23
bracelets and necklaces 5

diabetic foods 29

energy 6, 7, 14, 18
ethnic backgrounds 13
exercise 12, 24, 29
eye checks 22

famous people with diabetes 26–27
food choices 12, 20–21, 24, 29
friends 4, 16, 18, 23, 24–25

"going low" 18–19, 24, 29

helping people with diabetes 16, 23, 24

injections 14, 17
insulin 6, 7, 11, 14, 16, 17
insulin pump 15, 26

living with diabetes 14–17, 25

medical condition 4, 10

nerves 22
numbers of people with diabetes 28

overweight 12

people who get diabetes 8–9, 12–13

seizures 19
starchy foods 20
sugar 6, 7, 11, 14, 18, 19, 22, 23, 24, 29

tablets 16
Type 1 diabetes 7, 8–9, 14–15, 26, 27
Type 2 diabetes 10–11, 12–13, 16–17, 28

whole foods 21